Benchmark Assessments

mheducation.com/prek-12

Send all inquiries to:
McGraw-Hill Education
Two Penn Plaza
New York, New York 10121

ISBN: 978-0-07-906644-2
MHID: 0-07-906644-5

Printed in the United States of America.

4 5 6 7 8 9 LOV 25 24 23 22 21   C

Table of Contents

Benchmark Assessments

Benchmark Assessments is an integral part of the complete assessment program aligned with *Wonders,* state standards, and advances in summative assessment that feature performance-based tasks.

Purpose of *Benchmark Assessments*

The *Benchmark Assessments* component reports on the outcome of student learning and provides summative data in relation to progress through the curriculum. The results of the assessments can be used to inform subsequent instruction, aid in making leveling and grouping decisions, and point toward areas in need of reteaching or remediation. The tests in *Benchmark Assessments* are constructed to mirror the approach and subject concentration found in state-mandated end-of-year and performance-based assessments. Student performance in these assessments can act as a signal of student readiness for the demands of high-stakes testing as well as a snapshot of student progress toward end-of-year goals.

Focus of *Benchmark Assessments*

The tests focus on the following key areas of ELA:

- Comprehension of literature and informational text
- Using text features to access or clarify information
- Vocabulary acquisition and use
- Research skills
- Drafting, editing, and revising text
- Command of the conventions of standard English language
- Writing to sources within the parameters of specific genres

Assessment Items Featured in *Benchmark Assessments*

Benchmark assessments feature the following item types—selected response (SR), multiple selected response (MSR), evidence-based selected response (EBSR), constructed response (CR), technology-enhanced items (TE), and Performance Tasks (PT). (Please note that the print versions of TE items are available in this component; the full functionality of the items is available only through the online assessment.) This variety of item types provides multiple methods of assessing student understanding, allows for deeper investigation into skills and strategies, and provides students an opportunity to become familiar with the kinds of items and approaches they will encounter in high-stakes assessments.

Overview of *Benchmark Assessments*

The *Benchmark Assessments* component consists of three tests—Benchmark Test 1, Benchmark Test 2, and Benchmark Test 3.

Test 1 focuses on key skills that are part of the instruction in Units 1–3, Test 2 samples key skills from Units 1–6, and Test 3 features a suite of PTs.

Test 1 and Test 2 feature 30 items that mirror the focus and presentation students will encounter in end-of-year testing. The tests are broken into two sessions.

Test 3 contains examples of PTs that are part of traditional performance-based assessment.

- Narrative
  - Students craft a narrative using information from the sources.
- Informational
  - Students generate a thesis based on the sources using information from the sources to explain this thesis.
- Opinion
  - Students analyze the ideas in the sources and make a claim that they support using information from the sources.

Each PT assesses standards that address comprehension, research skills, genre writing, and the use of standard English language conventions (ELC). The stimulus texts and research questions in each task build toward the goal of the final writing topic.

Administering *Benchmark Assessments*

Benchmark Test 1 should be given to students after Unit 3 is completed. Benchmark 2 should be given to students close to the end of the year or before students take their EOY test. The PTs in Test 3 can be administered at various times during the year. The Narrative Task can be given at the start of the year and again closer to the performance-based assessment date to measure student growth and test readiness.

Due to the length of the test (and to provide students a test-taking experience that is in concert with standardized testing), the schedule below is suggested. (Session 1 and Session 2 can be spaced over two days or grouped together with a short break in between.)

- Session 1 of Tests 1 and 2—30 to 40 minutes
- Session 2 of Tests 1 and 2—30 to 40 minutes
- PTs in Test 3—90 to 100 minutes. (Provide students 30 to 40 minutes to read the stimulus materials and answer the research questions, and 60 to 70 minutes for planning, writing, and editing their responses. If desired, provide students a short break between these activities.)

Scoring *Benchmark Assessments*

Tests 1 & 2

Items 1–30 in Tests 1 and 2 are each worth two points, for a 60-point assessment. Each part of an EBSR is worth 1 point; MSR and TE items should be answered correctly in full, though you may choose to provide partial credit. For written responses, assign a score using the correct response parameters provided in the answer key and the scoring rubrics below.

Short Response Score 2: The response is well-crafted and concise and shows a thorough understanding of the underlying skill. Appropriate text evidence is used in the answer.

Short Response Score 1: The response shows partial understanding of the underlying skill. Text evidence is featured, though examples are too general.

Test 3

Each PT is a 15-point assessment. The three research items are worth a total of five points, broken down as indicated in the scoring charts. For PT full-writes, use the rubrics on the following pages. Score the task holistically on a 10-point scale: 4 points for purpose/ organization [P/O]; 4 points for evidence/elaboration [E/E] or development/elaboration [D/E]; and 2 points for English language conventions [C]. Unscorable or 0-point responses are unrelated to the topic, illegible, contain little or no writing, or show little to no command of the conventions of standard English. Use the anchor paper response provided for each PT for additional scoring guidance.

Evaluating Scores

The goal of each test is to evaluate student mastery of previously-taught material and to gauge preparedness for state-mandated testing.

Test 1 can serve as a summative, mid-year assessment.

Test 2 can serve as a summative, EOY assessment.

The PTs that comprise Test 3 can be assigned at points directly following specific instruction in the task genre to assess student mastery.

The expectation is for students

- to score 80% or higher on Tests 1 and 2; and
- to score "12" or higher on each PT.

For students who do not meet these benchmarks, assign appropriate lessons from the **Tier 2 online PDFs**. Use student results in particular test categories to guide intervention.

Teacher Introduction

NARRATIVE PERFORMANCE TASK SCORING RUBRIC

Score	Purpose/Organization	Development/Elaboration	Conventions
4	• **fully sustained** organization; **clear** focus • effective, unified plot • effective development of setting, characters, point of view • transitions clarify relationships between and among ideas • logical sequence of events • effective opening and closing	• **effective** elaboration with details, dialogue, description • clear expression of experiences and events • effective use of relevant source material • effective use of various narrative techniques • effective use of sensory, concrete, and figurative language	
3	• **adequately sustained** organization; **generally maintained** focus • evident plot with loose connections • adequate development of setting, characters, point of view • adequate use of transitional strategies • adequate sequence of events • adequate opening and closing	• **adequate** elaboration with details, dialogue, description • adequate expression of experiences and events • adequate use of source material • adequate use of various narrative techniques • adequate use of sensory, concrete, and figurative language	
2	• **somewhat sustained** organization; **uneven** focus • inconsistent plot with evident flaws • uneven development of setting, characters, point of view • uneven use of transitional strategies, with little variety • weak or uneven sequence of events • weak opening and closing	• **uneven** elaboration with **partial** details, dialogue, description • uneven expression of experiences and events • vague, abrupt, or imprecise use of source material • uneven, inconsistent use of narrative technique • partial or weak use of sensory, concrete, and figurative language	• **adequate** command of spelling, capitalization, punctuation, grammar, and usage • few errors
1	• **basic** organization; **little or no** focus • little or no discernible plot; may just be a series of events • brief or no development of setting, characters, point of view • few or no transitional strategies • little or no organization of event sequence; extraneous ideas • no opening and/or closing	• **minimal** elaboration with **few or no** details, dialogue, description • confusing expression of experiences and events • little or no use of source material • minimal or incorrect use of narrative techniques • little or no use of sensory, concrete, and figurative language	• **partial** command of spelling, capitalization, punctuation, grammar, and usage • some patterns of errors

INFORMATIONAL PERFORMANCE TASK SCORING RUBRIC

Score	Purpose/Organization	Evidence/Elaboration	Conventions
4	• **effective** organizational structure • clear statement of main idea based on purpose, audience, task • consistent use of various transitions • logical progression of ideas	• **convincing** support for main idea; **effective** use of sources • integrates comprehensive evidence from sources • relevant references • effective use of elaboration • audience-appropriate domain-specific vocabulary	
3	• **evident** organizational structure • adequate statement of main idea based on purpose, audience, task • adequate, somewhat varied use of transitions • adequate progression of ideas	• **adequate** support for main idea; **adequate** use of sources • some integration of evidence from sources • references may be general • adequate use of some elaboration • generally audience-appropriate domain-specific vocabulary	
2	• **inconsistent** organizational structure • unclear or somewhat unfocused main idea • inconsistent use of transitions with little variety • formulaic or uneven progression of ideas	• **uneven** support for main idea; **limited** use of sources • weakly integrated, vague, or imprecise evidence from sources • references are vague or absent • weak or uneven elaboration • uneven domain-specific vocabulary	• **adequate** command of spelling, capitalization, punctuation, grammar, and usage • few errors
1	• **little or no** organizational structure • few or no transitions • frequent extraneous ideas; may be formulaic • may lack introduction and/or conclusion • confusing or ambiguous focus; may be very brief	• **minimal** support for main idea; **little or no** use of sources • minimal, absent, incorrect, or irrelevant evidence from sources • references are absent or incorrect • minimal, if any, elaboration • limited or ineffective domain-specific vocabulary	• **partial** command of spelling, capitalization, punctuation, grammar, and usage • some patterns of errors

Teacher Introduction

OPINION PERFORMANCE TASK SCORING RUBRIC

Score	Purpose/Organization	Evidence/Elaboration	Conventions
4	• **effective** organizational structure; **sustained** focus • consistent use of various transitions • logical progression of ideas • effective introduction and conclusion • clearly communicated opinion for purpose, audience, task	• **convincing** support/evidence for main idea; **effective** use of sources; **precise** language • comprehensive evidence from sources is integrated • relevant, specific references • effective elaborative techniques • appropriate domain-specific vocabulary for audience, purpose	
3	• **evident** organizational structure; **adequate** focus • adequate use of transitions • adequate progression of ideas • adequate introduction and conclusion • clear opinion, mostly maintained, though loosely • adequate opinion for purpose, audience, task	• **adequate** support/evidence for main idea; **adequate** use of sources; **general** language • some evidence from sources is integrated • general, imprecise references • adequate elaboration • generally appropriate domain-specific vocabulary for audience, purpose	
2	• **inconsistent** organizational structure; **somewhat sustained** focus • inconsistent use of transitions • uneven progression of ideas • introduction or conclusion, if present, may be weak • somewhat unclear or unfocused opinion	• **uneven** support for main idea; **partial** use of sources; **simple** language • evidence from sources is weakly integrated, vague, or imprecise • vague, unclear references • weak or uneven elaboration • uneven or somewhat ineffective use of domain-specific vocabulary for audience, purpose	• **adequate** command of spelling, capitalization, punctuation, grammar, and usage • few errors
1	• **little or no** organizational structure or focus • few or no transitions • frequent extraneous ideas are evident; may be formulaic • introduction and/or conclusion may be missing • confusing opinion	• **minimal** support for main idea; **little or no** use of sources; **vague** language • source material evidence is minimal, incorrect, or irrelevant • references absent or incorrect • minimal, if any, elaboration • limited or ineffective use of domain-specific vocabulary for audience, purpose	• **partial** command of spelling, capitalization, punctuation, grammar, and usage • some patterns of errors

Teacher Introduction

Answer Keys in *Benchmark Assessments*

The answer keys for Tests 1 and 2 have been constructed to provide you with the information you need to aid understanding student performance. These answer keys include correct answers, content focus, and complexity levels.

15	B, E	Main Idea and Key Details	DOK 2
16	D	Context Clues	DOK 2
17A	C	Main Idea and Key Details	DOK 2
17B	B	Main Idea and Key Details/Text Evidence	DOK 2

The scoring tables that follow the answer keys show distinct categories to pinpoint possible areas of intervention or enrichment.

Comprehension: Selected Response 1A, 1B, 2A, 2B, 5, 7A, 7B, 8A, 8B, 9, 10A, 10B, 15, 17A, 17B, 18, 19, 21A, 21B, 23A, 23B, 24	/28	%
Comprehension: Constructed Response 4, 20	/4	%
Vocabulary 3, 6A, 6B, 16, 22A, 22B	/8	%
Research 11, 12, 13, 14	/8	%
English Language Conventions 25, 26, 27	/6	%
Drafting, Editing, Revising 28, 29, 30	/6	%
Total Benchmark Assessment Test 1 Score	/60	%

The answer keys for Test 3 include correct answers and complexity levels. They also provide space for recording scores.

BENCHMARK ASSESSMENT TEST 3: Narrative Performance Task			
Question	**Answer**	**Complexity**	**Score**
1	B, D	DOK 3	/1
2	see below	DOK 3	/2
3	see below	DOK 3	/2
Story	see below	DOK 4	/4 [P/O] /4 [D/E] /2 [C]
Total Score			**/15**

SESSION 1
Read the poem. Then answer the questions.

If I Could Fly
by Claire Daniel

If I had wings like a bird,
Then I would rise and fly.
I would explore distant lands
And mountains that touch the sky.

5   First I'd fly to far-flung shores,
To feel what it's like to be free.
I would float on waves, dive for food,
And wink at the whales I see.

I'd fly away to the rainforest,
10 To find other birds like me.
With toucans, eagles, and parrots,
I'd laugh at monkeys in the trees.

Next I'd fly to the desert,
Soar past a cactus or two.
15 I might chase a snake or rabbit,
There's so much I could do.

GO ON →

Next I'd fly to the frozen north,
A white snowy owl with me.
Tossing snowballs at polar bears
20 Until it's best to flee.

After all this flying I'm tired,
I need sleep and rest.
Where should I lay my weary head?
Which location is best?

25 But I don't have wings after all,
I'm anchored to the ground.
I'll snuggle in my bed at home,
and dream of flying 'round.

GO ON →

1   The following question has two parts. First, answer part A.
     Then, answer part B.

     Part A: Which sentence **best** describes what the second stanza
     shows about the narrator of the poem?

     A   The narrator wants to go on a trip.

     B   The narrator enjoys whale watching.

     C   The narrator enjoys studying the ocean.

     D   The narrator wants to be able to travel anywhere.

     Part B: Which line from the poem **best** supports your answer
     in part A?

     A   First I'd fly to far-flung shores,

     B   To feel what it's like to be free.

     C   I would float on waves, dive for food,

     D   And wink at the whales I see.

GO ON →

2   The following question has two parts. First, answer part A. Then, answer part B.

Part A: Which sentence **best** tells the message of the poem?

A   The author wishes she were a bird.

B   The author wishes she could see different animals.

C   The author wishes she were able to travel the world.

D   The author wishes she had more dreams of being a bird.

Part B: Which line from the poem **best** supports your answer in part A?

A   If I had wings like a bird,

B   I would explore distant lands

C   With toucans, eagles, and parrots,

D   and dream of flying 'round.

GO ON →

3 Complete the chart to match each phrase from the poem with its meaning. Mark **one** box under **each** phrase.

	"touch the sky"	"far-flung shores"	"feel what it's like to be free"	"anchored to the ground"
able to explore	☐	☐	☐	☐
very tall	☐	☐	☐	☐
unable to try new things	☐	☐	☐	☐
a great distance away	☐	☐	☐	☐

4 How does the last stanza add to the central idea of the poem? Use details from the poem to support your answer.

_____

_____

_____

_____

_____

GO ON →

Read the passage. Then answer the questions.

Marine Animals

The walrus is only one animal that lives in the sea but can also live on land.
It grows a thick coat to keep warm when it swims in the sea.

If you wanted to explore the ocean, you would need special equipment. A boat could take you over the water, but underwater is a different story. You would need special gear, such as air tanks, to let you breathe. In cold water, you would need a special suit to keep you warm.

Marine animals live in oceans without any gear at all. Their bodies have changed, or adapted, over the years to survive in many different places.

The Vast Oceans

Oceans cover over half of Earth's surface. More than one million different kinds of animals and plants live in the oceans. These animals have adapted in amazing ways.

Large animals, such as whales, need large areas to live in. For example, a blue whale can weigh 100 to 150 tons. When feeding, it can eat four tons of food each day! To find enough food, it travels thousands of miles each year. The blue whale needs a lot of space.

GO ON →

Surviving in Salty Water

Have you ever had a drink of salty water? Not only does it taste bad, it is not good for you. So how do animals live in it?

Marine fish have adapted to the salty water. Marine animals have specially developed kidneys, gills, and body functions that make sure their bodies are not harmed by too much salt. They can drink the water. Extra salt from the water is then pumped out of their gills.

Salt water also helps animals move and swim. Salt water is dense, so it makes floating easier. Huge animals like blue whales can move easily. They do not need big strong bones to support the weight of their huge bodies because the water does that.

Salt water actually presses down on animals that live beneath it. The deeper an animal swims, the more pressure the animal must withstand.

People can't dive in very deep water because the pressure is too great. Air in the lungs can be harmful, even dangerous. That is because the pressure of the water outside the body is much greater than the pressure inside. But many marine animals can dive down deep. Some push air out from their lungs as they dive. Another animal, the seal, has adapted in another way. Its lungs lose air like a flattened rubber bag. The air goes into the upper part of the seal's respiratory system. After its lungs collapse, the seal becomes heavier than the salt water. It sinks deeper and deeper.

Staying Warm

Ocean waters have different temperatures. Marine animals have adapted to the different temperatures in the oceans. Seals, walruses, and whales have developed layers of blubber, or fat.

The blubber protects the animal from the cold. The blubber on some whales can be as much as two feet thick!

GO ON →

Sea otters don't have blubber. Instead, they have adapted in a different way. They grow very thick fur. Their fur may have a million hairs per square inch! This thick fur doesn't allow the cold water to touch the skin.

Breathing Air

All animals must breathe, but marine animals do so in different ways. Fish have gills that take oxygen from the water. Other marine animals don't have gills. Whales and dolphins are two animals that must breathe air. They have to come to the surface of the water to breathe through blowholes on the tops of their heads.

Seals breathe air too, but they can hold their breath for a long time. Some can stay below the surface for over 30 minutes.

Blue Whales

Blue whales can't breathe underwater. Every few minutes they must come to the surface to take a breath. They blow out water and air and take in fresh air. Strong muscles around the blowholes close when the blue whale dives back down.

GO ON →

5   Read the paragraphs from the passage.

If you wanted to explore the ocean, you would need special equipment. A boat could take you over the water, but underwater is a different story. You would need special gear, such as air tanks, to let you breathe. In cold water, you would need a special suit to keep you warm.

Marine animals live in oceans without any gear at all. Their bodies have changed, or adapted, over the years to survive in many different places.

How does the second paragraph support the ideas in the first paragraph? Pick **two** choices.

A   It explains what kinds of animals live in the sea.

B   It reveals the main idea of the passage.

C   It describes how sea animals are able to live in the sea.

D   It names the tools that people can use to explore the sea.

E   It tells how people use special gear to learn more about the sea.

F   It compares how people and animals are suited for the places they live.

GO ON →

6 The following question has two parts. First, answer part A. Then, answer part B.

Part A: Read the sentence from the passage.

Its lungs lose air like a <u>flattened</u> rubber bag.

Which word **best** defines <u>flattened</u> as it is used in the sentence?

A   empty

B   large

C   soft

D   stretchy

Part B: Which sentence from the passage **best** supports your answer in part A?

A   "Air in the lungs can be harmful, even dangerous."

B   "Another animal, the seal, has adapted in another way."

C   "The air goes into the upper part of the seal's respiratory system."

D   "After its lungs collapse, the seal becomes heavier than the salt water."

GO ON →

7   The following question has two parts. First, answer part A. Then, answer part B.

Part A: What conclusion about the author's opinion is supported by the passage?

A   The ocean is difficult to learn about.

B   The ocean is filled with interesting animals.

C   The ocean is the best home for large animals.

D   The ocean is the most dangerous part of nature.

Part B: Which sentence from the passage **best** supports your answer in part A?

A   "Oceans cover over half of Earth's surface."

B   "These animals have adapted in amazing ways."

C   "Large animals, such as whales, need large areas to live in."

D   "Air in the lungs can be harmful, even dangerous."

GO ON →

8 The following question has two parts. First, answer part A. Then, answer part B.

Part A: What is the **most likely** reason the author uses a picture of a whale to illustrate the passage?

   A   because whales are the main topic of the passage

   B   because whales can be dangerous ocean animals

   C   because whales need very large areas of water to live in

   D   because whales have special parts that help them live in the ocean

Part B: Which detail from the passage **best** supports your answer in part A?

   A   "Large animals, such as whales, need large areas to live in."

   B   "When feeding, it can eat four tons of food each day!"

   C   "To find enough food, it travels thousands of miles each year."

   D   "They have to come to the surface of the water to breathe through blowholes on the tops of their heads."

GO ON →

9   The passage is divided into different sections. Complete the chart to match each section heading with its main idea. Mark **one** box under **each** heading.

	The Vast Oceans	Surviving in Salty Water	Staying Warm	Breathing Air
Animals are adapted to stay beneath the ocean waters for a long period of time.	☐	☐	☐	☐
Animals are adapted to travel long distances in ocean waters.	☐	☐	☐	☐
Animals are adapted for living in cold ocean waters.	☐	☐	☐	☐
Animals are adapted to drink and swim in ocean waters.	☐	☐	☐	☐

GO ON →

10 The following question has two parts. First, answer part A. Then, answer part B.

Part A: Which sentence **best** tells the main idea of the passage?

A People can explore the ocean using special equipment.

B People can find many interesting living things in the ocean.

C Animals that live in the ocean can breathe in different ways.

D Animals have special parts that help them live in the ocean.

Part B: Which sentence from the passage **best** supports your answer in part A?

A "If you wanted to explore the ocean, you would need special equipment."

B "Their bodies have changed, or adapted, over the years to survive in many different places."

C "More than one million different kinds of animals and plants live in the oceans."

D "All animals must breathe, but marine animals do so in different ways."

GO ON →

Read the directions. Then answer the questions.

11   A student is writing a research report about the benefits of recess.
      He wrote an opinion in the report. Read the sentences from the
      student's report and the directions that follow.

Recess is a very important time for students. Children need breaks
during a busy day of learning. Moving around can help students focus
better on what they are learning. A break can help students remember
the lessons better. Teachers need a break too. Some teachers use
stretches to give their students brain breaks.

The student took notes about the reasons kids need recess.
Choose **two** notes that support the student's opinion.

A   Teachers at schools without recess are usually unhappy.

B   Recess should be given to students who are well behaved.

C   Teachers who lead class stretches have more focused students.

D   Studies show students who have more breaks have
     better grades.

E   Schools where recess is given only as a reward have better
     behaved students.

F   Recess should be outside if possible and kids should not have
     electronic devices during this time.

GO ON →

12 A student is writing a research report about cell phones. She is looking for information about cell phone safety. Choose the **three** sentences that have information about cell phone safety.

A Many people began using cell phones in the 1990s.

B Using cell phones to text while driving is an increasing problem in our country.

C Some people fear that the waves sent out by cell phones could be harmful to humans.

D Now, with cell phones being so common, there are safety concerns people have about other electronic devices.

E Many people feel cell phones are helpful because you could always call for help in an emergency.

F Today cell phones have replaced almost every other type of phone, which means people have their phones wherever they go.

GO ON →

13 A student is writing a report about how chocolate is made. Which source would **most likely** have information for the report?

    A A website where people share their opinions of chocolate.

    B A magazine article about what happens inside chocolate factories.

    C A nonfiction book about how chocolate has changed over the years.

    D A medical journal study about the health benefits of eating chocolate.

14 A student is writing a report about bike safety. Which website is the **most useful** source of information for the report?

    A www.biketobehealthy.org

    B www.bikesandhelmets.org

    C www.bikesandgearsandchains.com

    D www.bikecrashstories.blogspot.com

SESSION 2

Read the passage. Then answer the questions.

A New Beginning

November 17, 1732

"It's the first day of our new life, Mercy," Mother said to me.
She's right. Today we're sailing out of London and toward America.
The ship is a busy place. The sailors don't care much for the passengers. They act like we're in the way. I want to be on deck all the time. There are so many ropes and sails, and so much water!

November 20, 1732

Gus, a gruff sailor, pulled me aside yesterday. This is his third trip west, he said. He also said that there are snakes as big as alligators where we are going. He said the mosquitoes are as big as ducks. He said I'd be lucky to last a week. I had nightmares last night. I wish we could go back home.

If truth be told, my family needs a change. My father is an excellent carpenter, but there are many excellent carpenters in London. He just never got enough work. Often we had little food. I was always outgrowing my shoes. So my father jumped at the opportunity to take his skills to a new country. We will all make a new start when we get to America.

We're sailing on the ship *Ann*. There are 115 of us. There are many families and children. I think there are too many of us.

Our quarters below deck are crowded and dark. Many passengers are seasick, even though the sailors tell us the seas are calm. I don't feel so well myself.

GO ON →

December 1, 1732

Dad built some shelves for the cook in the galley, so the sailors are friendlier to us. Gus took me up on the deck and showed me the ropes—except they aren't ropes after all. They are called "lines." This ship has hundreds of them. Gus showed me how they worked. I felt happy that he was teaching me all this, but then he started telling me about the Native Americans. He said they'd probably attack us when we reach land. That is, if the crocodiles didn't eat us first. I told my father what Gus said. He just laughed and said Gus was kidding with me.

December 15, 1732

I'm a terrible journal writer. I've just been so busy! I've been helping the sailors with the lines and sails. Gus is showing me how to use the stars to figure out which direction we are sailing. Today, I even got to go up to the crow's-nest! A ten-year old boy went first, and I was determined to go, too. I was really scared, but I am tired of being afraid. After I got up there, I was amazed at the ocean. There was dark blue water in every direction as far as I could see.

GO ON →

January 13, 1733

The good news is that we can now see land! We are docked in Charleston, South Carolina. The bad news is that we can't get off the boat yet. General Oglethorpe is going ashore to meet with the Native Americans so we can settle in a place just south of here.

It will be called Georgia. Oglethorpe, as we call him, named our town Savannah. Of course, there is nothing there yet!

February 12, 1733

We are here at last! There are tall bluffs instead of a beach. Groups of trees are on top of the cliffs. Oglethorpe says that is where we will build our town.

My mom keeps saying, "Look at all the trees!" Of course, when my dad sees trees, he sees benches, tables, chairs, and wooden houses.

I also noticed that there were no Native Americans waiting to attack us. There were no crocodiles lining up on the beach to eat us. I asked Gus where the mosquitoes and snakes were, and he said they were hiding in the bushes. I smiled. I told him I'd go into the woods and bring him some to take back to London.

GO ON →

15 The following question has two parts. First, answer part A. Then, answer part B.

Part A: Why did the author choose to describe how the narrator was feeling in the journal entries throughout the passage?

A   to show that the narrator changes her attitude

B   to show how unhappy the narrator was on her journey

C   to explain how lucky the narrator was to move to America

D   to explain that it was scary for the narrator to leave London

Part B: Which sentence from the passage **best** supports your answer in part A?

A   "Our quarters below deck are crowded and dark."

B   "If truth be told, my family needs a change."

C   "He said they'd probably attack us when we reach land."

D   "I was really scared, but I am tired of being afraid."

GO ON →

16 The following question has two parts. First, answer part A. Then, answer part B.

Part A: What conclusion about the narrator's father is supported by the passage?

A He is excited about their new start.

B He is sad they have to leave their home.

C He wishes they could get there faster.

D He is worried about being on the ship.

Part B: Which sentence from the passage **best** supports your answer in part A?

A "My father is an excellent carpenter, but there are many excellent carpenters in London."

B "So my father jumped at the opportunity to take his skills to a new country."

C "Dad built some shelves for the cook in the galley, so the sailors are friendlier to us."

D "Of course, when my dad sees trees, he sees benches, tables, chairs, and wooden houses."

GO ON →

17 The following question has two parts. First, answer part A. Then, answer part B.

Part A: Read the sentence from the passage.

He also said that there are snakes <u>as big as alligators</u> where we are going.

What does the author tell the reader about Gus by using the phrase "as big as alligators"?

A   Gus was trying to scare the narrator.

B   Gus had never really been to America.

C   Gus did not know much about the sizes of animals.

D   Gus wanted to get the narrator excited about America.

Part B: Which sentence from the passage **best** supports your answer in part A?

A   "Gus, a gruff sailor, pulled me aside yesterday."

B   "This is his third trip west, he said."

C   "I had nightmares last night."

D   "I wish we could go back home."

GO ON →

18 The following question has two parts. First, answer part A. Then, answer part B.

Part A: What conclusion can be drawn about how the narrator feels at the end of the passage?

  A She feels excited.

  B She feels curious.

  C She feels brave.

  D She feels proud.

Part B: Which sentence from the passage **best** supports your answer in part A?

  A "We are here at last!"

  B "There are tall bluffs instead of a beach."

  C "Of course, when my dad sees trees, he sees benches, tables, chairs, and wooden houses."

  D "I told him I'd go into the woods and bring him some to take back to London."

GO ON →

19 Which sentences **best** tell the main idea of the passage? Pick **two** choices.

    A "The ship is a busy place."

    B "If truth be told, my family needs a change."

    C "My father is an excellent carpenter, but there are many excellent carpenters in London."

    D "We will all make a new start when we get to America."

    E "He just laughed and said Gus was kidding with me."

    F "I'm a terrible journal writer."

20 The narrator uses several vocabulary words to describe the different parts of a ship. Explain the meanings of the words deck, galley, and quarters. Use details from the passage to support your answer.

_____

_____

_____

_____

_____

_____

GO ON →

Read the passage. Then answer the questions.

Our Nearest Neighbor

The Moon is Earth's closest companion. It is about 239,000 miles (384,000 kilometers) away from Earth. The diameter of the Moon is about 2,160 miles (3,476 kilometers). You can see it in the sky on most nights. Sometimes it is so bright that it lights up the night. The Moon does not make its own light. The sun shines on the Moon. We see the sunlight as it reflects back to us.

How Was the Moon Formed?

No one is completely sure how the Moon was formed. However, many scientists agree on one idea. They believe that long ago, Earth hit another planet and a chunk of Earth broke off. That chunk is now the Moon.

How Does the Moon Affect Us?

The Moon actually affects many events on Earth. The Moon is very heavy. This heavy mass of rock has gravity, a force that pulls things toward its center.

Earth has gravity too. Earth's gravity keeps your feet on the ground. It pulls you back to the ground when you jump. The Moon's gravity is much less than Earth's. You could jump much higher if you were on the Moon. But even though the Moon's gravity is not as strong as Earth's, it is strong enough to do other things.

The Moon's gravity pulls on Earth. It is not strong enough to pull Earth toward it, but it is strong enough to pull the water in the oceans. That is why we have tides. As the Moon pulls on the water, oceans rise and fall.

Tides are easy to see if you stand on a beach. When the tide rises, the water comes closer into shore. When it falls, the water flows away from the shore.

GO ON →

The Moon's Surface

The surface of the Moon is quite harsh. It is either very cold or very hot. There is no air to breathe. There is no wind. It has no running water. There are no plants or living things there. It would not be a very comfortable place to live. Still, the Moon is our neighbor, and we want to know as much about it as we can.

Moon Facts

This illustration shows Buzz Aldrin, the second person to walk on the Moon.

- Twelve people have walked on the Moon.
- The first spacecraft to reach the Moon was called Luna 2 and was from Russia. It landed in 1959.
- Astronauts have left footprints on the Moon. Since there is no wind on the Moon, the footprints will stay there for thousands of years.
- The first American spacecraft called Ranger 4 landed on the Moon in 1962.

GO ON →

How Much Do Things Weigh on the Moon?

Weight on Earth (in pounds)	Weight on the Moon (to nearest pound)
40	7
50	8
60	10
75	12
100	17
120	20
150	25

The Moon Today

Several countries, including India, China, Japan, and the United States, continue to explore the Moon. As we further develop our knowledge, we plan to have Americans return to the Moon by the year 2020.

In the future, scientists hope to send humans to other planets, like Mars. The Moon could be an ideal place to launch other missions. The Moon could help us learn more about space and other planets than we have even known before.

GO ON →

21 The following question has two parts. First, answer part A. Then, answer part B.

Part A: Which sentence **best** tells the main idea of the passage?

A The Moon has less gravity than Earth.

B The Moon is important to people on Earth.

C The Moon would not be a good place to visit.

D The Moon causes the oceans to rise and fall.

Part B: Which sentence from the passage **best** supports your answer in part A?

A "The Moon actually affects many events on Earth."

B "The Moon's gravity is much less than Earth's."

C "As the Moon pulls on the water, oceans rise and fall."

D "It would not be a very comfortable place to live."

GO ON →

22 The following question has two parts. First, answer part A. Then, answer part B.

Part A: Read the sentences from the passage.

Several countries, including India, China, Japan, and the United States, continue to explore the Moon. As we further develop our knowledge, we plan to have Americans return to the Moon by the year 2020.

Which phrase **best** states the meaning of explore as it is used in the sentences?

A look at

B talk about

C learn about

D wander over

Part B: Which phrase from the passage **best** supports your answer in part A?

A "As we further develop our knowledge"

B "Americans return to the Moon"

C "send humans to other planets"

D "launch other missions"

GO ON →

23 The following question has two parts. First, answer part A. Then, answer part B.

Part A: Why is looking at the table titled "How Much Do Things Weigh on the Moon?" important to understanding information about the Moon?

A   It shows that the Moon is smaller than Earth.

B   It shows that the Moon weighs less than Earth.

C   It shows that the Moon has less gravity than Earth.

D   It shows that the Moon is more dangerous than Earth.

Part B: Which feature of the table titled "How Much Do Things Weigh on the Moon?" **best** supports your answer in part A?

A   the title

B   the number of rows

C   the column headings

D   the increase of numbers by ten

24 Which sentence **best** describes how the feature called "Moon Facts" adds to the central idea of the passage?

A   It provides an illustration of the moon.

B   It provides a summary of the passage.

C   It provides a history of people going to the moon.

D   It provides answers to questions readers might ask.

GO ON →

Student Name _____

Read the directions. Then answer the questions.

25   Read the sentences from a student's story.

Jana enjoys walking along the beach. She likes looking for shells. The beach has many shells hidden in the sand. Her favorite shells ____ on a shelf in her bedroom.

Which word **best** complete the blank in the final sentence?

A   go

B   goes

C   going

26   Choose the word from the box that correctly completes each sentence. Write **one** word in **each** blank.

feet   tooth   foot   teeth

Jana dipped her right _____ into the cold ocean.

She spotted a dolphin about twenty _____ from the shore.

She saw a beautiful shark _____ in the water.

Jana made a necklace with all the shark _____ she found.

GO ON →

27 Which sentence does **not** have any errors in grammar?

A "What a beautiful shell?" exclaimed Jana.

B "Don't step on that jellyfish!" shouted Jana.

C "We're almost at the beach?" Jana said excitedly.

D "please let us stay longer." Jana begged her parents.

GO ON →

28 A student is writing an opinion article about dogs for her school newspaper. Read the draft of the article and complete the task that follows.

Many people own dogs. They are the best pets in the world. They are the best pets because they can be trained and taught tricks. People train them to obey commands such as sit, stay, and come. Some dogs learn to play dead and some even learn how to dance on their back legs. Dogs quickly become companions or friends with their owners. They enjoy going on walks with them, cuddling with them, and even riding in cars with them. Dogs are also loyal to their owners. They will follow them wherever they go.

Write a paragraph that concludes the article and supports the opinion about dogs.

_____

_____

_____

_____

_____

GO ON →

29   A student is writing a story for class about being in the rain. The student wants to revise the draft to add details. Read the draft and complete the task that follows.

Yesterday I took the bus on my way home from school and it started raining. My first thought was, "I don't have an umbrella!" As I climbed down the bus steps I could feel the raindrops falling on my head. Quickly my hair was getting soaked. <u>I was carrying a pile of library books for my book report.</u> I had to come up with a plan to keep them dry until I got home. First I took off my coat and wrapped them inside. Next, I put my body over the coat and started running home. As I was running, I tripped over a rock and fell on top of my coat and the books. Lucky for me my plan to wrap them up kept them dry.

Choose the **best** sentence to add **after** the <u>underlined</u> sentence to explain what is happening.

A   This morning I ran out of the house without my backpack.

B   Tomorrow the librarian would be very angry about these books.

C   I still had to walk two blocks to my house from the bus stop.

D   The bus driver started yelling at me to hurry up and get off the bus.

GO ON →

30 A student is writing an article for class about how to wash dishes. The student wants to revise the draft to make the directions clearer. Read the draft of the article. Then complete the task that follows.

Have you ever learned to wash dishes? It is a simple chore that can be done to help out around the house. First, you make sure the drain in your sink is closed. Place the dishes in the sink. You begin to fill the sink with hot water and add dishwashing soap. Then, using a sponge, begin scrubbing the leftover food off the dishes. Place the cleaned dishes on the rinsing side of the sink. After all the dishes are cleaned, turn on the water, and begin rinsing the soap off the dishes.

Choose the **best** way to connect the <u>underlined</u> sentences.

A Also,

B But,

C Finally,

D Next,

Benchmark Assessments

SESSION 1

Read the passage. Then answer the questions.

The Rabbit and the Well

Rabbit and his friends were busy weeding their garden plot. Soon, delicious lettuce, peas, and tomatoes would fill their lunch tables. However, Rabbit was more than lazy. His muscles were stretched-out rubber bands, and he was so hot that he thought his fur was on fire. He looked around to figure out a plan to get out of all that work. Then he had an idea.

"OW!" he cried. "A briar stuck me in the nose."

All of the animals gathered around Rabbit. Bear was the most sympathetic. He said, "You need to put some water on it."

So Rabbit took a walk, far away from all the work. Pretty soon he saw a well in the shade. He looked at the bucket at the top of the well. It was a perfect place to take a snooze, so he hopped into the bucket. The other pail at the bottom of the well didn't have much water in it. Rabbit's weight plunged the pail to the bottom of the well. Meanwhile, the other pail sailed up to the top.

Rabbit took a long drink from the water in the well. He relaxed near the chilly water and snoozed for a while, feeling quite comfortable. But then he realized that he was in a bind. How could he ever get out of the well? It was very dark, and the water was deep.

Fox followed Rabbit, guessing that he hadn't been stuck with a briar. Now he peered down the well. "What are you doing down there?" Fox yelled down to Rabbit.

"Not much," Rabbit said. But when he saw Fox's interest, he developed a clever plan.

GO ON →

"Tell me the truth," Fox said. "I know you're too smart to be down there doing nothing."

"I was here for a drink. But then, after closer inspection, I found fish down here." Rabbit knew that Fox loved fish.

"You've caught fish?"

"Yes," lied Rabbit, "Jump in the bucket and come on down. There's more than enough fish."

Fox jumped into the bucket. He was much heavier than Rabbit, so he crashed down to the bottom. On his way down, he passed Rabbit and saw his empty bucket and realized he had been fooled! Seconds later, Fox was stuck at the bottom of the well.

A little later, a farmer came to the well for water. You can imagine his surprise when he pulled up a fox in the bucket instead of water! When Fox saw the farmer, he ran away as fast as he could.

Back at the garden, Rabbit and Fox didn't say anything about their adventure. Then they started to laugh so hard that they fell on the ground and tears ran down from their eyes.

They might not trust each other, but they had both taken a crazy trip to the bottom of a well and lived to tell the tale.

GO ON →

1   The following question has two parts. First, answer part A. Then, answer part B.

Part A: Which of these conclusions about Rabbit is **best** supported by the passage?

A   Rabbit is very smart.

B   Rabbit is a good friend.

C   Rabbit is too tired to work.

D   Rabbit is sorry for tricking Fox.

Part B: Which of these sentences from the passage **best** supports your answer from part A?

A   "His muscles were stretched-out rubber bands, and he was so hot that he thought his fur was on fire."

B   "He relaxed near the chilly water and snoozed for a while, feeling quite comfortable. But then he realized that he was in a bind."

C   "But when he saw Fox's interest, he developed a clever plan."

D   "Then they started to laugh so hard that they fell on the ground and tears ran down from their eyes."

GO ON →

2 The following question has two parts. First, answer part A. Then, answer part B.

Part A: Which of the following **best** tells the lesson of the passage?

A Many hands can make light work.

B Always look first before you leap.

C Work now so that you can play later.

D Treat others as you would like to be treated.

Part B: Which sentence from the passage **best** supports your answer in part A?

A "Rabbit and his friends were busy weeding their garden plot."

B "Bear was the most sympathetic."

C "On his way down, he passed Rabbit and saw his empty bucket and realized he had been fooled!"

D "They might not trust each other, but they had both taken a crazy trip to the bottom of a well and lived to tell the tale."

GO ON →

3   The following question has two parts. First, answer part A. Then, answer part B.

Part A: Read the sentence from the passage.

But then he realized that he was in a bind.

What does "in a bind" mean?

A   to be tied up

B   to be confused

C   to have an injury

D   to have a problem

Part B: Which sentence from the passage **best** supports your answer in part A?

A   "It was a perfect place to take a snooze, so he hopped into the bucket."

B   "The other pail at the bottom of the well didn't have much water in it."

C   "How could he ever get out of the well?"

D   "Fox followed Rabbit, guessing that he hadn't been stuck with a briar."

GO ON →

4   Read the paragraphs from the passage.

Rabbit and his friends were busy weeding their garden plot. Soon, delicious lettuce, peas, and tomatoes would fill their lunch tables. However, Rabbit was more than lazy. His muscles were stretched-out rubber bands, and he was so hot that he thought his fur was on fire. He looked around to figure out a plan to get out of all that work. Then he had an idea.

"OW!" he cried. "A briar stuck me in the nose."

What conclusion can be drawn about why the author began the passage this way? Use details from the passage in your answer.

_____

_____

_____

_____

_____

_____

GO ON →

Read the passage. Then answer the questions.

Butterflies and Moths

The luna moth is light green with spots of yellow, and the wings are trimmed in bright blue.

The monarch butterfly is bright orange, yellow, white, and black.

During the summer months, butterflies and moths fly about in the warm air. They are in the same insect family. The Lepidoptera family's name means "scale wing." That's because their wings are covered in tiny scales. If you have ever picked up a butterfly or moth, you might notice that you get "dust" on your fingers. This dust is made from the tiny scales.

How Butterflies and Moths are Similar

Both butterflies and moths lay eggs. The shells of their eggs are usually very hard, to protect them from being eaten by birds or other animals. After the eggs hatch, they become caterpillars.

GO ON →

After eating a lot of food, most caterpillars make a cocoon. The caterpillar stays inside the cocoon and slowly changes. It is now called a pupa. When it breaks out of the cocoon, the pupa has become a butterfly or moth.

You can find these insects wherever plants grow. However, adult butterflies and moths do not eat plants. Adult butterflies lay their eggs close to plants because this is the food caterpillars eat.

Most caterpillars eat leaves and flowers. Adult moths and caterpillars drink nectar from flowers. They also suck minerals from mud.

Moths and butterflies also have the same enemies. Spiders enjoy eating these flying insects. Bats and birds also eat them.

Life Cycle of a Butterfly

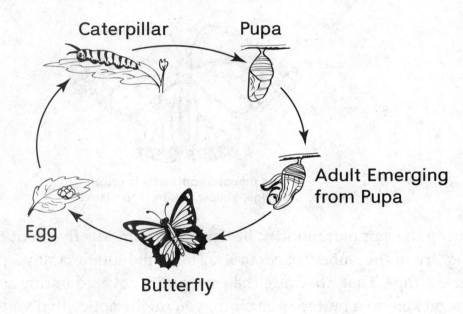

GO ON →

Telling Butterflies and Moths Apart

Moths and butterflies have a lot of similarities, but they are also very different. You might notice that you only see butterflies during the day. This is the main time they are active. However, moths are active mostly at night. Many moths are attracted to light. A good place to find these moths is around lights, windows, and doors. Butterflies are very brightly colored. They can be all colors of the rainbow, from blue to orange to black. Moths can be brightly colored, too. But most of them are not. The reason they have less color is so their enemies will not see them during the daytime. Most moths tend to be brownish or white, but some are different colors. The luna moth is light green and looks like a leaf.

Moths have more scales than butterflies. This makes them look almost furry. Moths also have thicker bodies. These extra scales and thickness help keep them warm at night.

To see the biggest difference in butterflies and moths, you have to look very closely. Butterflies and moths do not have noses. They have two antennae. Butterflies and moths use these to smell. These feelers stick out from the front of their bodies. If you look closely at the antennae on the two insects, you will see differences. Moth antennae are feather-like and pointed at the end. Butterfly antennae have knobs on the end.

The Importance of Butterflies and Moths

Most people love butterflies. However, some people do not think highly of moths. They think moths are pests. The truth is, butterflies and moths are both important to plants. The adults help fruits and vegetables grow. After they sip nectar from flowers, they carry tiny bits of pollen on their bodies. As they go from flower to flower, they spread this pollen. Pollen is a powder. Without pollen, fruits and vegetables would not grow. Without moths and butterflies, we would not have as much to eat.

GO ON →

5 The following question has two parts. First, answer part A. Then, answer part B.

Part A: Which conclusion about moths and butterflies is supported by the passage?

A Moths and butterflies are brightly colored.

B Moths and butterflies have similar antennae.

C Moths and butterflies are important to plants.

D Moths and butterflies are active during the day.

Part B: Which sentence from the passage **best** supports your answer in part A?

A "This is the main time they are active."

B "Most moths tend to be brownish or white, but some are different colors."

C "Butterfly antennae have knobs on the end."

D "The adults help fruits and vegetables grow."

GO ON →

6 The following question has two parts. First, answer part A. Then, answer part B.

Part A: Look at the diagram titled "Life Cycle of a Butterfly." What conclusion about the life cycle is supported by the diagram and the passage?

A Caterpillars break out of the pupa or cocoon.

B Caterpillars eat the eggs laid by the butterfly.

C The caterpillar changes to a pupa in the cocoon.

D The caterpillar lays eggs in the second life stage.

Part B: Which sentence from the passage **best** supports your answer in part A?

A "After the eggs hatch, they become caterpillars."

B "After eating a lot of food, most caterpillars make a cocoon."

C "When it breaks out of the cocoon, the pupa has become a butterfly or moth."

D "Adult butterflies lay their eggs close to plants because this is the food caterpillars eat."

GO ON →

7 The following question has two parts. First, answer part A. Then, answer part B.

Part A: Which sentence **best** describes the main idea of the passage?

A Butterflies and moths go through stages.

B Most kinds of butterflies and moths have many colors.

C The eggs of butterflies are easy for other animals to eat.

D Butterflies want their eggs to be eaten as part of the life cycle.

Part B: Which sentence from the passage **best** supports your answer in part A?

A "The shells of their eggs are usually very hard, to protect them from being eaten by birds or other animals."

B "The caterpillar stays inside the cocoon and slowly changes."

C "Adult butterflies lay their eggs close to plants because this is the food caterpillars eat."

D "Moths can be brightly colored, too."

GO ON →

Student Name _____

8 Decide whether the detail from the passage describes butterflies, moths, or both. Mark **one** box for **each** detail.

	butterflies	moths	both
wings are made of tiny scales	☐	☐	☐
many are attracted to light	☐	☐	☐
eggs are very hard	☐	☐	☐
antennae have knobs on the end	☐	☐	☐

9 Read the sentence from the passage.

When it breaks out of the cocoon, it has become a butterfly or moth.

Which words mean almost the same as the word breaks?
Pick **two** choices.

A bursts

B drips

C erupts

D moves

E unfolds

GO ON →

10 What conclusion about the author's point of view is supported by the passage?

   A The author wants to convince the reader that both moths and butterflies are pretty.

   B The author wants to warn the reader to be careful when touching butterflies or moths.

   C The author wants to entertain the reader with interesting facts about butterflies and moths.

   D The author wants to tell the reader that both moths and butterflies help make the food we eat.

GO ON →

Read the directions. Then answer the questions.

11 A student is writing a research report about sports. He found a source. Read the source and the directions that follow.

Source 1

Sports are a great way to stay active and learn many life skills. There are many sports to choose from and many can be played throughout the year. Not only do you exercise your body but also your mind. Playing a sport helps you set goals for yourself and your team. You learn that if you don't practice then you won't get better. Sports teach you how to listen to adults with respect. You learn to follow directions. Playing a sport gives you an opportunity to meet different people. Quickly, you will make new friends. You also learn to work with others and be part of a team. Once you find the sport that you love, you will begin to become more confident. It teaches you to work hard in everything you do. But above all, it keeps your body moving!

The student took notes about sports. Choose **two** notes that support the author's opinion in the source.

A Sports can be for everyone.

B Sports are a way to learn more.

C You can play sports at any time.

D You can choose from many sports.

E Sports help your body stay healthy.

F You must play sports to improve your skills.

GO ON →

12   A student is writing a research report about sports. She took notes and thought of four main ideas for her report. Draw lines to match **each** main idea with its supporting detail.

Main Ideas	Supporting Details
Sports can be social.	While playing sports, you make connections with others.
Sports are all about effort.	While playing sports, you are taught to follow steps.
Sports exercise your mind.	To be your best at a sport you have to work at it.
Sports teach you things.	See the play in a sport and decide on your next move.

13   A student has made a plan for research. Read the plan and the directions that follow.

Research Report Plan
Topic: St. Louis
Audience: other students
Purpose: to inform
Research Question: How has St. Louis changed in the past 100 years?

A student is writing a report about the city of St. Louis. Which website is the **most useful** source of information for the report?

A   www.stlouistodaymagazine.com

B   www.stlouispostnewspaper.com

C   www.stlouisvacations.org

D   www.stlouistodayandyesterday.org

GO ON →

14 A student has made a plan for research. Read the plan and the directions that follow.

Research Report Plan
Topic: wild cats
Audience: students
Purpose: to inform
Research Question: Where are wild cats located around the world?

A student is writing a report about wild cats. Which book would **most likely** have information for the report?

A How to Train Your Cat

B The Wild Animals of Africa

C How to Survive in the Wild

D The History of Cats in America

SESSION 2

Read the passage. Then answer the questions.

The Three Cranes: A Chinese Folktale

Once there was a wise old man named Tian who lived in the mountains. He lived with three black cranes. He fed and loved the birds, and they were devoted to him. The birds often flew to the village. When they returned, they told Tian of the people who lived below. Tian was troubled by the stories because people were not kind to one another. He knew he had to leave the mountain to share his wisdom.

On the way to the village, he passed a beggar and asked to exchange clothes. The beggar said, "I cannot do this. You are wearing fine red silk robes. I am only wearing rags." Tian insisted, and the beggar agreed. Tian wandered along the streets of the village and asked for food and money, but no one helped. Those who did notice him taunted him. "Only a lazy man would be as poor as you," people said. Others yelled, "Get a job, useless beggar!"

One evening Tian stopped at an inn and knocked on the door. An innkeeper named Wang answered and said, "What can I do for you?" Tian said, "Could you give me some food? I'm very hungry, but I have no money to pay you." Wang said, "You are welcome here. Come in and share my food and drink." Wang gave him soup, tea, and rice. Soon Tian's belly was full.

The next day Tian returned and asked Wang again for food. From then on, Tian returned day after day and Wang continued to feed him. After a few months, Tian came for his last meal. When he had finished, he said, "Now it is time that I repay you."

GO ON →

Wang said, "Nonsense! I gladly give you food and drink." Tian ignored the man and took a brush out of his knapsack. Then he painted three cranes on the wall of the inn. Next, he took out a flute and began playing. The cranes stepped off the wall and began dancing to the tune. Wang turned to Tian. He said, "Who are you that you can do such things?" But Tian just smiled and waved goodbye. The cranes returned to the wall.

When music played in the inn, the cranes left the wall and danced. Word of the dancing cranes spread like wildfire. More and more came to see the cranes. No matter how busy Wang became, he always kept a bowl of soup for the needy.

A year later, Tian returned to the inn. Wang said, "Look what has happened! Your cranes have made me as rich as a king! How can I ever repay you?

Tian said, "There is one way. Just teach others what you have learned. Life is a schoolroom. Show others what you know about kindness, and that will repay me."

The three cranes flew onto the outstretched arm of Tian as he said goodbye. The cranes lifted Tian off the floor and carried him back up toward the mountaintop. Wang realized that the beggar was the Lord of the Cranes. For the rest of his life, Wang told this story to all who would listen. In this way, he repaid his debt.

GO ON →

15 The following question has two parts. First, answer part A. Then, answer part B.

Part A: What is the theme of the passage?

A   Give to everyone.

B   Be nice to others.

C   Rich people should give to the needy.

D   Older people should share their wisdom.

Part B: Which sentence from the passage **best** supports your answer in part A?

A   "Tian was troubled by the stories because people were not kind to one another."

B   "No matter how busy Wang became, he always kept a bowl of soup for the needy."

C   "'Your cranes have made me as rich as a king!'"

D   "Wang realized that the beggar was the Lord of the Cranes."

GO ON →

16 The following question has two parts. First, answer part A. Then, answer part B.

Part A: What conclusion about Tian is supported by the passage?

A He knew cranes are magical birds.

B He knew debts should always be repaid.

C He knew wisdom is needed in our world.

D He knew kindness is important to have.

Part B: Which sentence from the passage **best** supports your answer in part A?

A "Once there was a wise old man named Tian who lived in the mountains."

B "Tian was troubled by the stories because people were not kind to one another."

C "When he had finished, he said, 'Now it is time that I repay you.'"

D "When music played in the inn, the cranes left the wall and danced."

GO ON →

17 The following question has two parts. First, answer part A. Then, answer part B.

Part A: How does the second paragraph add to the central idea of the passage?

A   It shows how unselfishly people lived.

B   It shows how badly people were treated.

C   It shows how highly people thought of Tian.

D   It shows how people thought Tian was wealthy.

Part B: Which detail from the passage **best** supports your answer in part A?

A   "On the way to the village, he passed a beggar and asked to exchange clothes."

B   "'You are wearing fine red silk robes.'"

C   "Tian insisted, and the beggar agreed."

D   "Those who did notice him taunted him."

GO ON →

18 The following question has two parts. First, answer part A. Then, answer part B.

Part A: Read the sentence from the passage.

Word of the dancing cranes <u>spread like wildfire</u>.

What does the author mean by the phrase "spread like wildfire"?

A   traveled across many miles

B   burned down homes of unkind people

C   rapidly caused people to seek safety

D   quickly became known by many people

Part B: Which sentence from the passage **best** supports your answer in part A?

A   "Tian wandered along the streets of the village and asked for food and money, but no one helped."

B   "From then on, Tian returned day after day and Wang continued to feed him."

C   "More and more came to see the cranes."

D   "Wang said, 'Look what has happened!'"

GO ON →

19 How does Tian solve his problem in the passage? Make a checkmark in one box for the problem and one box for the solution.

	Tian's Problem	Tian's Solution
could not repay the innkeeper	☐	☐
told people about the dancing cranes	☐	☐
knew people were not nice to each other	☐	☐
dressed like a beggar to find someone kind	☐	☐

20 What can the reader conclude about Wang in paragraph 3? Use details from the passage to support your answer.

_____

_____

_____

_____

_____

GO ON →

Read the passage. Then answer the questions.

Margaret Knight, Inventor

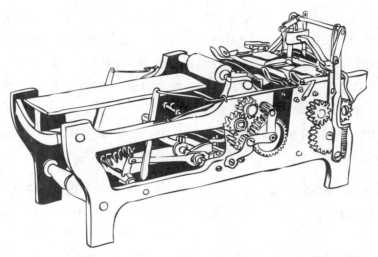

Knight's machine folded and glued the bottom of paper bags.

When you think of famous inventors, what names come to mind? Do you think of Alexander Graham Bell, who invented the telephone? Maybe you think of Thomas Edison, inventor of the light bulb. But do you ever think of Margaret Knight? Perhaps not, but she was actually one of the invention giants of her day.

Early Ideas

Margaret Knight was born in 1838 in Maine. She was an unusual young girl, and she loved building things. When she was only 12 years old, she saw a bad accident in a cotton mill. A worker was injured. Young Margaret made a tool that would shut off a machine if something got caught in it. Several years later, the tool was used in mills. This tool is still used today in cotton mills.

The Paper Bag and the Villain

Knight's best-known invention was the modern paper bag. In 1868, Knight was working in a plant that made flat paper bags. These bags were like envelopes and would only lie flat. Knight had an idea. She wanted to make a bag that would stand up so items could be packed inside it. However, making

GO ON →

these bags by hand would cost too much. So she worked on an idea for a new bag. This one would have a bottom and stand up. Then she designed a machine that would assemble the paper bags cheaply. The machine cut, folded, and glued the bag together.

After she made the machine, she applied for a patent. That is a paper saying that she owned the idea. Anyone who wanted to use her idea would have to pay her for it. A man named Charles Annan wanted credit for Knight's idea. So Annan took Knight to court. He said that he invented the machine. His only reason was because he said it was impossible for a woman to invent such a machine! In those days, women did not usually invent things. But Knight had proof of her invention.

She had written and drawn plans for her idea. Because she was able to show the plans to the court, she won the case. From 1871 on, stores began to buy Knight's bags.

The Paper Bag Business

Next, Knight set up a company called the Eastern Paper Bag Company. This company made paper bags and sold them. It used Knight's machines. One machine could do the work of 30 people.

Today, paper bags are still made with machines that are based on Knight's design. They can make 200 to 650 sacks each minute! There are over 7,000 of these machines all over the world. These bags are still used in grocery stores and many other stores. Every American home probably has at least one of these bags.

More Inventions

Knight did not stop with the invention of the paper bag. She invented many more things. One was a machine that cut out the shapes of shoes. Another was a window frame. She invented a machine that would sew. She also invented a rotary engine.

Knight died in 1914. Before she died, she had created somewhere between 80 and 100 inventions. She had about 20 patents. Even though Margaret Knight is not well known, she was an important inventor.

GO ON →

21 The following question has two parts. First, answer part A. Then, answer part B.

Part A: What conclusion can be made based on the passage?

A A lot of women were unknown inventors at that time.

B Men did not create as many inventions as women at that time.

C Some people did not think women should be inventors at that time.

D The courts allowed only men to hold patents on inventions at that time.

Part B: Which sentence from the passage **best** supports your answer in part A?

A "Perhaps not, but she was actually one of the invention giants of her day."

B "Anyone who wanted to use her idea would have to pay her for it."

C "A man named Charles Annan wanted credit for Knight's idea."

D "His only reason was because he said it was impossible for a woman to invent such a machine!"

GO ON →

22 The following question has two parts. First, answer part A. Then, answer part B.

Part A: Read the sentence from the passage.

Then she designed a machine that would <u>assemble</u> the paper bags cheaply.

Which phrase **best** defines <u>assemble</u> as it is used in the sentence?

A to build

B to fold

C to invent

D to meet

Part B: Which sentence from the passage **best** supports your answer in part A?

A "These bags were like envelopes and would only lie flat."

B "So she worked on an idea for a new bag."

C "This one would have a bottom and stand up."

D "The machine cut, folded, and glued the bag together."

GO ON →

23 What is the author's purpose for writing the passage?
Pick **two** choices.

    A   to explain who Margaret Knight was

    B   to explain how paper bags are made

    C   to explain how inventors can get a patent

    D   to explain all of Margaret Knight's inventions

    E   to explain how Margaret Knight was unusual for her time

    F   to explain that people can get injured when working in a mill

24 What is the **most likely** reason the author included an illustration in the passage?

    A   to show an example of a famous invention

    B   to show one of Margaret Knight's many inventions

    C   to show why paper bags are made with a machine

    D   to show how Margaret Knight came up with new ideas.

GO ON →

Read the directions. Then answer the questions.

25   A student is writing a story for class. Read the paragraph from her story.

The bald eagle lived in the tallest pine tree in the woods. One day I went to look for his nest with Grandma. Grandma and I like to hike in the woods because it is interesting. Grandma had _____ his nest last year.

Which word **best** completes the final sentence?

A saw

B see

C seen

D sees

26   Read the paragraph from a student's story.

We went down the muddy path, and I was glad I wore hiking boots because my feet were dry. I wanted to keep walking to where I thought the eagle would be, _____ Grandma told me to stop. She pointed up to the tree where a very large nest was sitting.

Choose the word that **best** fills in the blank and connects the sentences.

A and

B but

C so

D or

GO ON →

27 Which of the following sentences is written correctly?

    A Me saw a huge nest at the very top of the tree.

    B Grandma gave me she binoculars so I could see better.

    C Inside were baby bald eagles chirping for they're mother.

    D Grandma and I had found the bald eagle and her babies.

GO ON →

28 A student is writing a report for her class about sleep. Read the draft of the report and complete the task that follows.

Every living thing needs to sleep, especially you! After a busy day at school, your body needs to rest. Sleep also helps to repair your body if you are sick or injured. You may feel tired and cranky if you don't get enough sleep. When you sleep, your brain gets a chance to sort through all the information from the day.

You can help your body get the sleep it needs. One way is to not watch TV or eat in bed. It's a good idea to start winding down early in the evening to help your body get ready for sleep. You should follow the same routine every night.

Write a paragraph that concludes the student's paper.

_____

_____

_____

_____

_____

GO ON →

29 A student is writing a story for her music class about a recent performance. The student wants to revise the draft to show the order of events. Read the draft of the story and complete the task that follows.

I was so nervous. My knees were shaking as I approached the stage. My stomach was in knots thinking about what was about to happen. My fingers still ached from practicing. At last the time had come for me to show everyone what I had learned. I smoothed the wrinkles out of my new dress. Time seemed to go by so slowly as I waited for my turn. I grabbed my music, and I walked in front of the audience. All of a sudden, I felt my feet trip underneath me and I dropped my instrument. While trying to keep it from hitting the floor, I let go of my music, which went flying through the air. The audience stopped clapping and everyone was silent. I picked myself up and gathered my music. I could feel that my face was red. I wanted to run and hide, but I had been practicing for too long to quit. I took a deep breath and began playing.

Choose the **best** sentence to support how the underlined sentences show that time changes.

A Finally, the backstage manager gave me my signal.

B Next, I paced back and forth backstage and hummed to myself.

C After all, all the performers were told to look their best for this night.

D At first, my entire family was in the audience waiting for me to perform.

GO ON →

30 A student is writing an opinion article about exercise for her class. The student wants to revise the draft to add a strong conclusion. Read the draft of the opinion article and complete the task that follows.

Students should take time every day to exercise. Exercise makes your heart stronger. By working out your heart, it does a better job of pumping oxygen to your cells. Exercise can also make your body stronger and more flexible. This can help you perform better at sports. Exercise can help you to stay healthy as well. It's also fun to exercise with friends.

Some people say that exercising your brain is just as important. By doing "brain games" you can improve your concentration, memory, or focus. You can do crossword puzzles, brain teasers, or Sudoku to get a mental workout.

Choose the sentence that would make the **best** conclusion for the article.

A Your brain needs just as much exercise as your body.

B Exercise is equally important for your body and your mind.

C Exercising can help you think more clearly after a long day at school.

D You can get your friends involved in exercising with you to make it more fun as well.

Narrative Performance Task

Task:

Your class has been learning about how animals protect themselves. Your teacher has explained how animals have their own clever ways of staying safe. You decide to do some more research on the topic. While doing your research, you read two sources.

After you have reviewed these sources, you will answer some questions about them. Briefly scan the sources and the three questions that follow. Then, go back and review the sources carefully to gain the information you will need to answer the questions and complete your research.

In Part 2, you will write a story using information from the two sources.

Directions for Part 1

You will now review two sources. You can review any of the sources as often as you like.

Research Questions:

After reviewing the research sources, use the rest of the time in Part 1 to answer three questions about them. Your answers to these questions will be scored. Also, your answers will help you think about the information you have read and viewed, which should help you write your story. You may also look at your notes.

GO ON →

Source #1: Hiding in Camouflage

In the animal world, there is one rule. It says, "Eat or be eaten." Some animals can fly or run away from danger. Other animals use a trick to hide themselves. It's called camouflage. Animals use their body color to hide. They also use their body shape to stay safe.

Color Change

Animals use their fur color to stay out of sight. They may also use their feathers or scales to hide. The birds in the forest use their brown feathers to hide in trees. Some animals can change colors. They are one color when they are young. Then as they grow older, the color of their fur changes. The color may change because they are now hunters. An animal's color also changes with the seasons. For example, the Arctic fox is dark during the summer. The fox's dark color blends in with the land around it. In winter, the fox's fur turns white. It blends in with the snow that covers the ground. It makes it harder for other animals to find it in the snow. Some insects can change colors in seconds. They sense danger and their color changes.

Many kinds of sharks are gray, and dolphins are grayish blue. These colors help the animals blend in with the water. Most deer and squirrels are brownish gray. Their colors help them stay hidden in the forest. A grasshopper is green to blend in with the grass and other plants.

Color Patterns

Some animals use their spots or stripes to hide. These patterns make it easier for animals to look like the things around them. For example, the zebra's coat is a pattern of stripes. In a herd of zebras, the white and black stripes all blend in together. The zebras look like one huge animal rather than just one zebra. A hungry lion has trouble seeing just one zebra in a group like that. Another animal that hides is the tiger. Its stripes help it hide in the tall grass.

GO ON →

Two Colors

Animals with two different colors can also trick other animals. They might have one color on their stomachs and another color on their backs. The two colors help them blend into many places in the forest. A red squirrel uses its reddish brown color to look like the forest ground. When the squirrel is in a tree it uses its white belly to look like the sky.

Body Shape

Another type of camouflage is when an animal uses its body shape to stay out of danger. While walking among trees, you may never see the walking stick. Its body looks like a branch. The praying mantis is another animal that looks like a branch. Grasshoppers hide in the grass and look like leaves.

Next time you are walking in the forest look for those animals that are hiding. Some may be using color to hide. Some may be using shape to hide.

GO ON →

Source #2: Animal Defenses

The animal world can be dangerous. Some animals will run from danger. Some animals will fight back. Still others have different ways of defending themselves. Animals have to fight back to keep themselves from harm. Harm could mean death.

Some Animals Run

What will some animals do when they sense danger? Some animals will run. Yes, some will just run fast. Others have a special way of running away. The deer will first lift its white tail to warn others. Then it will start running left to right at a high speed. The deer hopes to confuse the animal chasing it.

Rabbits are also runners. They run away in a back-and-forth pattern. It makes it hard to follow them. Both deer and rabbits hope the other animal will give up. Ducks will fly away from danger. Some ducks will jump up and start flying. Other ducks walk fast and then use their wings to fly. Once in the air, they are safe.

Some Animals Attack

Some animals will attack when they are in danger. The skunk first warns other animals by lifting its tail. It is the skunk's way of saying, "Back off!" Then it sprays a smelly mist in the direction of the threat. The mist can be smelled for miles. It has a horrible scent.

Another animal that uses spray as a defense is the bombardier beetle. If it senses danger, it will mix chemical liquids that come from its body and fill its back end with those liquids. Then it sprays the liquid from its tail with a loud popping sound. Not only is the spray smelly, it is also boiling hot. Watch out!

On the other hand, a bee uses its stinger. It will buzz to let others know it's around. If threatened, it will sting to protect itself.

GO ON →

Unique Animals

Did you know that some animals play dead? Well, they do. The opossum will fall over and curl up if threatened. Its tongue will hang out of its mouth. Once playing dead, the opossum hopes the other animal will lose interest and walk away.

Another great defense is puffing up the body. A toad will puff up its whole body to look about three times its normal size to keep predators away. Once bigger, it scares the other animal.

Two other unique animals are the worm and the turtle. It is not easy to tell one side of a worm from another. If a bird or other animal takes the back end of a worm, it can grow a new end. The worm gets a second chance at staying alive. The turtle has the best protection: its shell. If an animal tries to attack it, the turtle can pull all of its body parts into the shell. It stays safe. Teeth or claws cannot destroy a turtle's shell.

How amazing are animals? Each one has ways of hunting, ways of eating, and ways of staying alive. There is so much to learn about animals.

GO ON →

1   "Hiding in Camouflage" gives information about how animals
    protect themselves with the colors and shapes of their bodies.
    Choose **two** details from "Animal Defenses" that give **different**
    information about the ways animals protect themselves.

    A   Sharks tend to be gray in color.

    B   Most squirrels can be two colors.

    C   Animals run to stay safe and avoid harm.

    D   Survival in the animal world is never easy.

    E   Walking sticks are hard to find in the forest.

    F   Some animals will spray a mist to stay out of danger.

2   Both sources discuss how animals protect themselves. What
    does "Hiding in Camouflage" explain about how animals protect
    themselves that "Animal Defenses" does not? Explain why that
    information is helpful for the reader. Give **two** details from "Hiding
    in Camouflage" to support your answer.

    _____

    _____

    _____

    _____

    _____

    _____

GO ON →

3   Explain why animals can be sneaky. Give **two** reasons, one from
"Hiding in Camouflage" and one from "Animal Defenses." For each
reason, include the source title.

_____

_____

_____

_____

_____

_____

GO ON →

Directions for Part 2

You will now review your notes and sources, and plan, draft, revise, and edit your story. You may use your notes and go back to the sources. Now read your assignment and the information about how your story will be scored; then begin your work.

Your teacher has asked the class to write about what has been taught on how animals protect themselves. You decide to write a story about an animal protecting itself.

Your Assignment:

Your assignment is to write a story about an animal in the forest who encounters an enemy. Write a story that is several paragraphs long about what happens to the animal. Writers often do research to add interesting details to the setting, characters, and plot in their stories. Be sure to use the information that you learned about in the sources when you write about your animal encounter. Make sure your story includes a setting, gives information about the characters, and tells what happens. Remember to use words that describe and don't just tell. Your story should have a clear beginning, middle, and end.

REMEMBER: A well-written story

- has a clear plot and clear sequence of events.
- is well-organized and has a point of view.
- uses details from the sources to support your story.
- uses clear language.
- follows rules of writing (spelling, punctuation, and grammar usage).

Now begin work on your story. Manage your time carefully so that you can plan, write, revise, and edit the final draft of your story. Write your response on a separate sheet of paper.

Informational Performance Task

Task:

Your class is creating a book about unique animals and insects. Each person has been assigned to learn about one kind of animal that helps people. Your assignment is to learn about silkworms. While doing your research, you have found two sources.

After you have reviewed these sources, you will answer some questions about them. Briefly scan the sources and the three questions that follow. Then, go back and read the sources carefully so you will have the information you will need to answer the questions and complete your research.

In Part 2, you will write an informational article using information from the two sources.

Directions for Part 1

You will now review two sources. You can review any of the sources as often as you like.

Research Questions:

After looking at the sources, use the rest of the time in Part 1 to answer three questions about them. Your answers to these questions will be scored. Also, your answers will help you think about the information you have read, which should help you to write your informational article. You may refer to the sources when you think it would be helpful. You may also look at your notes.

GO ON →

Source #1: Silk Moths

Have you ever seen a silk moth? There are a few different kinds. The giant silk moth is the largest moth in North America. Silk moths have a soft body covered in fine hairs. They have two pairs of wings. These wings are covered in tiny scales. The scales give the moth its color. Silk moths are mostly brown, orange, and white. Moths usually rest during the day. They are active at night, or nocturnal.

Silk moths begin their lives as small eggs. In the spring, the female moth lays eggs in a tree, which is often a mulberry tree. These eggs are bright yellow like a lemon. After about ten days, the eggs turn black. The tiny caterpillars, or silkworms, are ready to emerge. After the silkworms hatch, they eat leaves from the trees. They nibble on these leaves for a few weeks. As the silkworms eat leaves, they grow larger. They may molt, or shed, their outer skin once or twice as they eat and grow.

Next, the silkworms spin silky cocoons around themselves. Some kinds of silkworms make such nice cocoons that their silk is used to make cloth.

The silkworms spend the winter in their cocoons. Finally, in the spring, they break out of their cocoons. They are now moths. Adult moths don't really have teeth or mouths, so they do not eat. Silk moths will live only long enough to mate and lay eggs. Even though they have wings, they cannot even fly. After the silk moths lay their eggs, they die. Then the cycle of life begins again.

GO ON →

Source #2: The Secret of Silk

How long do you think you could keep a secret? Do you think you could keep a secret for more than 3,000 years? The Chinese people did.

According to Chinese legend, a princess was walking in her garden one day. Suddenly, something fell into her teacup. Plop! She peered into her cup. She saw that a cocoon had fallen into it. As she pulled the cocoon out of her cup, a long shiny thread pulled free from it. It was the most beautiful thread she had ever seen. She caught her breath. She imagined herself wearing a dress woven from this magic thread. It was silk!

The princess learned how to raise silkworms. She shared the secret with her people. They learned to feed the small silkworms mulberry leaves until they grew fat and made a cocoon. They found out that if they kept the silkworm from emerging from the cocoon, they could unwind it. This way they were able to get long, unbroken threads. They combined the threads so they became thick and strong. They used these threads to weave cloth.

The Chinese people used this cloth to make beautiful clothes. At first only very rich people wore these silk clothes. These clothes were wonderful because they kept you warm in cold weather. They kept you cool in the summer. They used dye to make the shiny clothes brightly colored. Soon everyone wanted to wear silk.

People far and wide heard about silk. They journeyed far across the desert to trade gold, gems, or spices for silk cloth. The path that they took through the Chinese desert became known as the Silk Road. The road was filled with danger. Many travelers crossed it anyway. Caravans of people rode camels across the harsh desert. They faced sandstorms, robbers, hunger, and thirst. Why would anyone want to take these risks? If the caravans made it to China they could get silk. These people could make a lot of money for the silk if they could bring it back to their country.

GO ON →

The Chinese were very careful to keep their secret. People from everywhere wanted to know how to make silk. The Chinese would not tell. Anyone who tried to leave China with silkworms, or tell the secret of making silk was punished. They grew very rich from selling and trading their silk. It was a secret worth keeping.

One day some old men came to China. The men caught silkworms. They hid them inside of their walking sticks. They took the silkworms back to their country. There, they learned how to make the cocoons into silk. The secret was out!

GO ON →

1   Look at the details below. Mark **one** box next to **each** detail to
     show whether it belongs in "Silk Moths," "The Secret of Silk," both
     sources, or neither source.

	Source #1: Silk Moths	Source #2: The Secret of Silk	Both sources	Neither source
Silkworms have a short life cycle.	☐	☐	☐	☐
Raising silkworms is difficult.	☐	☐	☐	☐
Silkworm cocoons are used to make cloth.	☐	☐	☐	☐
Silk was very rare and expensive.	☐	☐	☐	☐

2   Explain which source has the most helpful information in
     understanding why silk was so important to people. Support your
     answer with **two** details from your chosen source.

_____

_____

_____

_____

_____

GO ON →

3   Both sources discuss the topic of silkworms. What does "Silk
    Moths" explain about silkworms that the "The Secret of Silk"
    does not? Explain why that information is helpful to the reader.
    Give **two** details from "Silk Moths" to support your answer.

_____

_____

_____

_____

_____

_____

GO ON →

Directions for Part 2

You will now review your notes and sources, and plan, draft, revise, and edit your writing. You may use your notes and go back to the sources. Now read your assignment and the information about how your writing will be scored; then begin your work.

Your Assignment:

Your class has been learning about unique animals and insects and is now ready to create a book about the topic. For your part in the book, you are going to write an informational article about silkworms. Your article will be read by other students, teachers, and parents.

Using both sources, develop a main idea about how the silk moth's life cycle affects how silk is made. Choose the most important information from the sources to support your main idea. Then, write an informational article that is several paragraphs long. Clearly organize your article and support your main idea with details from the sources. Use your own words except when quoting directly from the sources. Be sure to give the source title when using details from it.

REMEMBER: A well-written informational article

- has a clear main idea.
- is well-organized and stays on the topic.
- has an introduction and conclusion.
- uses details from the sources to support your main idea.
- puts the information from the sources in your own words except when using direct quotations.
- gives the title or number of the source.
- uses clear language.
- follows rules of writing (spelling, punctuation, and grammar usage).

Now begin work on your article. Manage your time carefully so that you can plan, write, revise, and edit the final draft of your article. Write your response on a separate sheet of paper.

STOP

Opinion Performance Task

Task:

Your class has been learning about endangered animals. Your teacher has asked the class to think about which animal needs the most protection, the peregrine falcon or sharks. You decide to do more research on both animals. As part of your research, you have found two sources.

After you have reviewed these sources, you will answer some questions about them. Briefly scan the sources and the three questions that follow. Then, go back and read the sources carefully so you will have the information you will need to answer the questions and complete your research.

In Part 2, you will write an opinion paper using information from the two sources.

Directions for Part 1

You will now look at two sources. You can look at either of the sources as often as you like.

Research Questions:

After reviewing the sources, use the rest of the time in Part 1 to answer three questions about them. Your answers to these questions will be scored. Also, your answers will help you think about the information you have read, which should help you write your opinion paper. You may refer to the sources when you think it would be helpful. You may also look at your notes.

GO ON →

Source #1: Saving the Peregrine Falcon

The peregrine falcon flies faster than any other bird. It can reach speeds of more than 200 miles an hour! The bird uses this speed to snatch its food with its strong claws when it is flying. Bird lovers have been interested in this special bird for a long time. It almost disappeared more than 50 years ago.

The Disappearance of the Peregrine Falcon

Starting in 1950, farmers began using a chemical called DDT. They put this chemical on crops to kill insects. About six years later, people noticed that many animals were dying, including the peregrine falcon. Then, in 1962, an expert named Rachel Carson wrote a book called *Silent Spring*. This book explained how harmful chemicals like DDT could be to the environment. These chemicals were killing the animals that ate the insects.

For example, the chemical made the peregrine falcon's eggs thin and brittle. When the females sat on their eggs to warm them, the eggs cracked. No baby chicks were born. There were fewer peregrine falcons each year. Scientists studied the chemicals, and they agreed with Rachel Carson. Then starting in 1973, harmful chemicals such as DDT were no longer allowed to be used in the United States.

GO ON →

Protecting the Peregrines

Peregrine falcons are strong fliers. They can fly thousands of miles in a year. Even though the United States did not allow the use of DDT, some other countries still used it. Peregrines could still eat animals that contained the chemical from other places. To protect the birds, scientists took some adult birds to a nursery to lay their eggs. Then they took the chicks to safe places. There the chicks could safely grow into adults.

Scientists chose Acadia National Park as one of the safe places. In 1984, scientists brought the bird to the park. In two years, they brought 22 chicks there when they were three or four weeks old. The park is a good place for the peregrines because it has high mountain ledges where the birds like to live. The birds were placed outside in a wooden box for three more weeks. They were fed food and water from a long tube. This meant that the chicks would not have contact with people. The chicks learned to live in their new home. Finally, they began to hunt for food on their own. When it was time to lay their eggs, they built nests at this site.

A Success Story

The first eggs from the replaced chicks hatched in 1991. From 1991 to 2011, at least 87 chicks have hatched in the park. Both Canada and the United States have worked hard to save peregrine falcons. Today, the peregrine falcon is back and stronger than ever. In some places, there are more peregrines than there were 60 years ago. For scientists and bird lovers, the story of the peregrine falcon is a success.

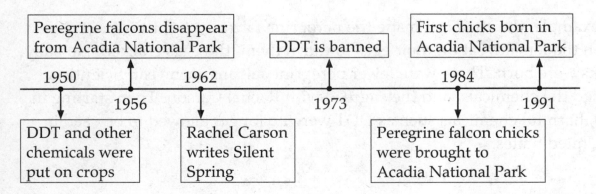

GO ON →

Source #2: Endangered Sharks

Did you know that some wildlife organizations believe that one-third of all sharks may become extinct? Many scientists believe that about 100 million sharks are caught and killed each year.

Even though scientists are worried about sharks becoming extinct, scientists can only estimate how many sharks are in the wild. This means they do not know the exact number of sharks there are. There may be many more sharks than we realize. Scientists might be wrong about how few sharks are in the wild. They might be wrong about how many sharks are caught.

Scientists do know that there are over 400 species of sharks in the world. Sharks might be anywhere from 6 inches to 40 feet long, depending on the species. Some species are considered endangered. Many species are threatened. Threatened species may become endangered soon.

Some sharks are caught as bycatch. This means that they are caught accidentally while fishing for something else. Other sharks are caught on purpose. Many sharks are caught for their fins. In some cultures, shark fin soup is considered a delicacy. So shark fins are worth a lot of money in these cultures. Sharks are used in many other items, too. These goods do not list shark on their ingredient lists. Instead, they use words like *squalene* and *shagreen*.

Many people want to protect the shark population. However, it takes a lot of time and money to work with sharks, and even more research is needed. Satellite tracking tags are sometimes used by scientists to learn about sharks. Equipment, such as tracking devices and shark cages, is expensive. There are other methods to research sharks, but all methods cost money and time.

Governments have to spend time creating shark protection laws and voting them into effect. But laws are not enough. Wildlife organizations that protect sharks need donations to help pay for their work. Saving sharks is an effort that depends on everyone, not just scientists.

GO ON →

1 Fill in the chart to show the idea supported by each source. Mark **one** box under **each** source.

	Source #1: Saving the Peregrine Falcon	Source #2: Endangered Sharks
Animals become extinct when their homes are destroyed by humans creating buildings and roads.	☐	☐
Some animals are caught and killed by accident.	☐	☐
Chemicals can harm animals even after countries ban their use.	☐	☐

GO ON →

2   Explain what the sources say about endangered animals. Use **one**
detail from **each** source to support your explanation. For each
detail, include the source title.

_____

_____

_____

_____

_____

3   Explain which source has the most useful information about how
to help protect animals. Support your answer with **two** details
from your chosen source.

_____

_____

_____

_____

_____

GO ON →

Directions for Part 2

You will now review your notes and sources, and plan, draft, revise, and edit your writing. You may use your notes and go back to the sources. Now read your assignment and the information about how your writing will be scored; then begin your work.

Your Assignment:

Your school is raising money for endangered and at-risk animals. People are not sure if the money should go to help peregrine falcons or sharks. Your teacher has asked you to write an opinion paper to share with the principal.

Your assignment is to convince your principal to use the money to help peregrine falcons or sharks. State your opinion clearly, and write several paragraphs that support it with reasons and details from the sources. Use your own words to develop your ideas, except when quoting directly from the sources. Be sure to give the source title for the details or facts you use.

REMEMBER: A well-written opinion paper

- has a clear opinion, is well-organized and stays on the topic.
- has an introduction and conclusion.
- uses details or facts from the sources to support your opinion.
- puts the information from the sources in your own words except when using direct quotations.
- gives the title or number of the source.
- develops ideas clearly.
- uses clear language.
- follows rules of writing (spelling, punctuation, and grammar usage).

Now begin work on your paper. Manage your time carefully so that you can plan, write, revise, and edit the final draft of your paper. Write your response on a separate sheet of paper.

Test 1 Answer Key

Student Name: _____

BENCHMARK ASSESSMENT TEST 1			
Question	Correct Answer	Content Focus	Complexity
1A	D	Point of View	DOK 3
1B	B	Point of View/Text Evidence	DOK 3
2A	C	Message/Lesson	DOK 2
2B	B	Message/Lesson/Text Evidence	DOK 2
3	see below	Context Clues: Sentence Clues	DOK 2
4	see below	Literary Elements: Stanza/Text Evidence	DOK 3
5	C, F	Text Structure: Sequence	DOK 3
6A	A	Context Clues: Sentence Clues	DOK 2
6B	C	Context Clues: Sentence Clues/Text Evidence	DOK 2
7A	B	Author's Point of View	DOK 2
7B	B	Author's Point of View/Text Evidence	DOK 2
8A	D	Text Features: Illustrations	DOK 2
8B	D	Text Features: Illustrations/Text Evidence	DOK 2
9	see below	Text Features: Headings	DOK 2
10A	D	Main Idea and Key Details	DOK 2
10B	B	Main Idea and Key Details/Text Evidence	DOK 2
11	C, D	Research	DOK 3
12	B, C, E	Research	DOK 3
13	B	Research	DOK 3
14	B	Research	DOK 2
15A	A	Point of View	DOK 3
15B	D	Point of View/Text Evidence	DOK 3
16A	A	Character, Setting, Plot: Character	DOK 2
16B	B	Character, Setting, Plot: Character/Text Evidence	DOK 2

BENCHMARK ASSESSMENT TEST 1			
Question	Correct Answer	Content Focus	Complexity
17A	A	Figurative Language: Metaphors and Similes	DOK 2
17B	C	Figurative Language: Metaphors and Similes/ Text Evidence	DOK 2
18A	A	Point of View	DOK 2
18B	A	Point of View/Text Evidence	DOK 2
19	B, D	Theme	DOK 2
20	see below	Context Clues: Sentence Clues/Text Evidence	DOK 2
21A	B	Main Idea and Key Details	DOK 2
21B	A	Main Idea and Key Details/Text Evidence	DOK 2
22A	C	Context Clues: Sentence Clues	DOK 2
22B	A	Context Clues: Sentence Clues/Text Evidence	DOK 2
23A	C	Text Features: Headings	DOK 2
23B	C	Text Features: Headings/Text Evidence	DOK 2
24	A	Text Features: Illustrations	DOK 2
25	A	Subject-Verb Agreement	DOK 1
26	see below	Singular and Plural Nouns	DOK 1
27	B	Commands and Exclamations	DOK 1
28	see below	Opinion: Drafting, Editing, Revising	DOK 3
29	C	Narrative: Drafting, Editing, Revising	DOK 3
30	D	Informational: Drafting, Editing, Revising	DOK 2

Comprehension: Selected Response 1A, 1B, 2A, 2B, 5, 7A, 7B, 8A, 8B, 9, 10A, 10B, 15A, 15B, 16A, 16B, 18A, 18B, 19, 21A, 21B, 23A, 23B, 24	/28	%
Comprehension: Constructed Response 4, 20	/4	%
Vocabulary 3, 6A, 6B, 17A, 17B, 22A, 22B	/8	%
Research 11, 12, 13, 14	/8	%
English Language Conventions 25, 26, 27	/6	%
Drafting, Editing, Revising 28, 29, 30	/6	%
Total Benchmark Assessment Test 1 Score	/60	%

3   • "touch the sky" - very tall
• "far-flung shores" - a great distance away
• "feel what it's like to be free" - able to explore
• "anchored to the ground" - unable to try new things

4   **2-point response:** The last stanza helps readers to understand that the author longs to be a bird for the freedom birds have to travel and explore. The author says that she is "anchored to the ground," which shows the author is disappointed that she cannot fly and feels stuck since she does not have the freedom of birds. However, the author also states that she will snuggle in her bed and "dream of flying 'round," which shows the author realizes that she has the freedom of birds when she dreams.

9   • "The Vast Oceans" - Animals are adapted to travel long distances in ocean waters.
• "Surviving in Salty Water" - Animals are adapted to drink and swim in ocean waters.
• "Staying Warm" - Animals are adapted for living in cold ocean waters.
• "Breathing Air" - Animals are adapted to stay beneath the ocean waters for a long period of time.

20   **2-point response:** The deck is out in the open. The story explains that it is where you can see the ropes, sails and water. The galley is like the kitchen of the ship. The story says it is where the cook can be found. The quarters are like rooms for those on the ship. The story says they are below the deck and are crowded and dark.

26   • Jana dipped her right <u>foot</u> into the cold ocean.

• She spotted a dolphin about twenty <u>feet</u> from the shore.

• She saw a beautiful shark <u>tooth</u> in the water.

• Jana made a necklace with all the shark <u>teeth</u> she found.

28   **2-point response:** Dogs are the best pets because they are smart. They can be trained. They are loyal companions to their owners.

Test 2 Answer Key

Student Name: _____

BENCHMARK ASSESSMENT TEST 2			
Question	Correct Answer	Content Focus	Complexity
1A	A	Character, Setting, Plot: Character	DOK 2
1B	C	Character, Setting, Plot: Character/Text Evidence	DOK 2
2A	B	Theme	DOK 2
2B	C	Theme/Text Evidence	DOK 2
3A	D	Figurative Language: Idioms	DOK 2
3B	C	Figurative Language: Idioms/Text Evidence	DOK 2
4	see below	Character, Setting, Plot: Sequence/Text Evidence	DOK 3
5A	C	Main Idea and Key Details	DOK 2
5B	D	Main Idea and Key Details/Text Evidence	DOK 2
6A	C	Text Features: Diagram	DOK 2
6B	C	Text Features: Diagram/Text Evidence	DOK 2
7A	A	Main Idea and Key Details	DOK 2
7B	B	Main Idea and Key Details/Text Evidence	DOK 2
8	see below	Text Structure: Compare and Contrast	DOK 2
9	A, C	Synonyms	DOK 2
10	D	Author's Point of View	DOK 2
11	B, E	Research	DOK 2
12	see below	Research	DOK 2
13	D	Research	DOK 2
14	B	Research	DOK 2
15A	B	Theme	DOK 3
15B	A	Theme/Text Evidence	DOK 3
16A	D	Point of View	DOK 3
16B	B	Point of View/Text Evidence	DOK 3

Test 2 Answer Key

Student Name: _____

BENCHMARK ASSESSMENT TEST 2			
Question	Correct Answer	Content Focus	Complexity
17A	B	Character, Setting, Plot: Sequence	DOK 3
17B	D	Character, Setting, Plot: Sequence/ Text Evidence	DOK 3
18A	D	Figurative Language: Metaphors and Similes	DOK 3
18B	C	Figurative Language: Metaphors and Similes/ Text Evidence	DOK 3
19	see below	Character, Setting, Plot: Problem and Solution	DOK 3
20	see below	Character, Setting, Plot: Character/ Text Evidence	DOK 3
21A	C	Author's Point of View	DOK 3
21B	D	Author's Point of View/Text Evidence	DOK 3
22A	A	Context Clues: Sentence Clues	DOK 2
22B	D	Context Clues: Sentence Clues/ Text Evidence	DOK 2
23	A, E	Author's Purpose	DOK 3
24	B	Text Features: Illustrations	DOK 3
25	C	Verb Tenses	DOK 1
26	B	Compound Sentences and Conjunctions	DOK 1
27	D	Pronouns	DOK 1
28	see below	Informational: Drafting, Editing, Revising	DOK 3
29	A	Narrative: Drafting, Editing, Revising	DOK 2
30	B	Opinion: Drafting, Editing, Revising	DOK 2

Comprehension: Selected Response 1A, 1B, 2A, 2B, 5A, 5B, 6A, 6B, 7A, 7B, 8, 10, 15A, 15B, 16A, 16B, 17A, 17B, 19, 21A, 21B, 23, 24	/28	%
Comprehension: Constructed Response 4, 20	/4	%
Vocabulary 3A, 3B, 9, 18A, 18B, 22A, 22B	/8	%
Research 11, 12, 13, 14	/8	%
English Language Conventions 25, 26, 27	/6	%
Drafting, Editing, Revising 28, 29, 30	/6	%
Total Benchmark Assessment Test 2 Score	/60	%

4 **2-point response:** The author began the story like this to show the reader how lazy rabbit is. He will do anything to avoid work. It also shows the reader that rabbit is very clever. He pretends to be stuck with a briar so he will not have to help in the garden.

8
- wings are made of tiny scales
  - both
- many are attracted to light
  - moths
- eggs are very hard
  - both
- antennae have knobs on the end
  - butterflies

12
- Sports can be social.
  - While playing sports, you make connections with others.
- Sports are all about effort.
  - To be your best at a sport you have to work at it.
- Sports exercise your mind.
  - See the play in a sport and decide on your next move.
- Sports teach you things.
  - While playing sports, you are taught to follow steps.

19
- Tian's Problem
  - knew people were not nice to each other
- Tian's Solution
  - dressed like a beggar to find someone kind

20 **2-point response:** The reader can tell that Wang is a generous person. He seems to care for all people, not just those who are paying customers. Tian announces that he cannot pay Wang and Wang still tells him he is welcome to eat at his inn. Wang doesn't just give him scraps either. He feeds him a full meal of rice, soup, and tea. Wang has probably fed other hungry beggars before. He does not think it is strange for Tian to ask to be fed without being able to pay, and provides him with a good meal. Wang's kindness and willingness to help a person in need show how generous he is.

28 **2-point response:** Sleep is an important part to staying healthy. Sleep helps your body repair itself. It also gives you more energy. You can help your body by getting the sleep you need.

BENCHMARK ASSESSMENT TEST 3: Narrative Performance Task			
Question	**Answer**	**Complexity**	**Score**
1	C, F	DOK 3	/1
2	see below	DOK 3	/2
3	see below	DOK 3	/2
Story	see below	DOK 4	/4 [P/O] /4 [D/E] /2 [C]
Total Score			/15

2   **2-point response:** "Hiding in Camouflage" explains and defines camouflage. Camouflage is when an animal uses its body color or shape to stay hidden from its enemies. This explanation of what camouflage is helps the reader understand that animals don't need to run away or attack to stay safe. They can use their own bodies to stay out of sight. "Hiding in Camouflage" states, "An animal's color also changes with the seasons." The Arctic fox has white fur in the winter to blend in with the snow and dark fur in the summer to blend in with the land. "Hiding in Camouflage" also states, "Another type of camouflage is when an animal uses its body shape to stay out of danger."

3   **2-point response:** Animals can be sneaky because they have ways to hide and watch without others knowing they are around. "Hiding in Camouflage" says that animals can use their spots and stripes to hide in tall grass and blend in with things around them. "Animal Defenses" states that some animals "play dead" hoping that their enemy will give up and leave them alone. This shows that some animals have ways of trying to trick their enemies.

10-point anchor paper: One cold, winter day, Papa Buck was getting ready to head out into the dark forest to search for food. It had been a long winter with very little to eat. He knew he had to get out into the forest early if he was going to find enough plants, leaves, or bushes for his family to eat. He told Mama Deer to wait about 10 minutes or so then follow behind him with Dawn Fawn. "Better be safe than sorry. I'll make sure it is safe to be in the forest," he said.

Papa Buck knew that now that their fur had darkened, they would not be easy to spot. Most all of the plants and trees had turned brown for the winter, and nothing was blooming. They would be able to blend in with the trees. Still, he was head of this deer family, and he had to protect them. Slowly, he crept out from behind the trees and started his search. As he was moving forward, he heard a twig snap. Quickly, he turned around to see a vicious wolf about 25 feet away staring back at him.

He was about to start running when he spotted Mama Deer behind the wolf. He immediately lifted his tail to warn her. She turned back and ran in the opposite direction. Papa Buck then began running in a zigzag pattern as the wolf ran after him. Papa Buck knew that up ahead was a group of houses with plenty of places to hide. Faster and faster he ran! Left, right! Left, right! As Papa Buck made a move right, he could see the wolf had stopped. How lucky! The wolf had come across some mice and decided to chase them instead. Quietly, Papa Buck trotted toward the trees he called home. He had escaped, and his family was safe.

Test 3 Answer Key

Student Name: _____

BENCHMARK ASSESSMENT TEST 3: Informational Performance Task			
Question	**Answer**	**Complexity**	**Score**
1	see below	DOK 3	/1
2	see below	DOK 3	/2
3	see below	DOK 4	/2
Informational Article	see below	DOK 4	/4 [P/O] /4 [E/E] /2 [C]
Total Score			**/15**

1   Source #1: Silk Moths - Silkworms have a short life cycle.
Source #2: The Secret of Silk - Silk was very rare and expensive.
Both sources - Silkworm cocoons are used to make cloth.
Neither source - Raising silkworms is difficult.

2   **2-point response:** "The Secret of Silk" is most helpful for understanding why silk was so important to people because it explains that silk was worth a lot of money. It also explains that silk was a wonderful material. In "The Secret of Silk," it says that "These people could make a lot of money for the silk if they could bring it back to their country." This source also explains that "These clothes were wonderful because they kept you warm in cold weather. They kept you cool in the summer."

3   **2-point response:** "Silk Moths" explains the appearance of the silk moth throughout its life cycle. This information is important to the reader because it helps the reader imagine and compare what the silk moth looks like when it is an egg, when it is a young caterpillar, when it is in its cocoon, and after it hatches. This source asks, "Have you ever seen a silk moth?" This source also explains the diet of the silk moth throughout its life cycle. It says that silkworms eat mulberry leaves until they get very fat. It also says, "Adult moths don't really have teeth or mouths, so they do not eat" so that the reader knows that once the silk moth emerges from the cocoon it does not eat at all because it only lives a short time.

10-point anchor paper: Silk seems like a magical material. According to "The Secret of Silk," it can keep you cool in the summer and warm in the winter. Silk comes from silkworms. Silkworms come from tiny eggs and hatch in the spring.

The source "Silk Moths" says that when silk moth eggs hatch, the silkworms eat mulberry leaves. People who use the silkworms to get silk have to feed them a lot of leaves. In "Silk Moths," it says that silkworms "may molt, or shed, their outer skin once or twice as they eat and grow."

Finally, when the silkworms have grown and grown, the "Silk Moths" source says that they "spin silky cocoons around themselves." In "The Secret of Silk" source, it says that if people "kept the silkworm from coming out, they could unwind the cocoon." People can then take the long strings from the cocoon to make silk thread. It also says in "The Secret of Silk" that the thread is combined together so that it can be used to weave silk cloth. If the silk moth breaks open the cocoon to become a moth, they cannot get the thread.

BENCHMARK ASSESSMENT TEST 3: Opinion Performance Task

Question	Answer	Complexity	Score
1	see below	DOK 3	/1
2	see below	DOK 3	/2
3	see below	DOK 4	/2
Opinion Paper	see below	DOK 4	/4 [P/O] /4 [E/E] /2 [C]
Total Score			**/15**

1   Source #1: Saving the Peregrine Falcon - Chemicals can harm animals even after countries ban their use.
Source #2: Endangered Sharks - Some animals are caught and killed by accident.

2   **2-point response:** Animals can become endangered for a lot of different reasons. In the "Endangered Sharks" article, the author says that sometimes sharks are caught accidentally as bycatch, but sometimes they are caught on purpose, especially for their fins. In the "Saving the Peregrine Falcon" article, the author says that the chemical DDT was causing the falcon to become endangered. Sometimes animals become endangered because people do not know that what they are doing can be harmful to animals. However, sometimes animals become endangered because people knowingly hurt them.

3   **2-point response:** "Saving the Peregrine Falcon" has the most helpful information in understanding how to help protect endangered animals. This source is most likely to help people understand what steps need to be taken to protect endangered animals because the steps taken to help the peregrine falcon have been considered a success. In the Peregrine Falcon article, the author says that "In some places, there are more peregrines than there were 60 years ago." The source also explains the steps that scientists took to help the peregrine. The author writes, "To protect the birds, scientists took some adult birds to a nursery to lay their eggs. Then they took the chicks to safe places." The article explains how scientists protected birds from the chemical DDT and then moved the chicks to safe places to continue to protect the species.

10-point anchor paper: Our school fundraiser to help endangered animals has caused some disagreement. Some people think we should use the money raised to help peregrine falcons. Other people think we should use the money raised to help save sharks. After learning about both peregrine falcons and sharks, I think we should use the money to help save sharks.

Peregrine falcons have already been considered a success story. In the article "Saving the Peregrine Falcon," the author states that "In some places, there are more peregrines than there were 60 years ago." Sharks, on the other hand, are currently threatened or endangered.

One possible reason that the peregrine falcons are considered a success but sharks are not might be that people know more about what is harming the falcons. They do not know all of the things that are harming and endangering sharks. "Saving the Peregrine Falcon" article says that DDT was a harmful chemical that hurt the birds. Many countries banned this chemical a long time ago. Also, because Rachel Carson wrote a book about it, people know that chemicals harm animals. In the "Endangered Sharks" article, there are several things listed that show how sharks are hurt. These things are happening right now. Things like shark finning, accidental bycatch, and using shark in products all hurt the number of sharks in the wild.

According to "Endangered Sharks," it is impossible for scientists to know exactly how many sharks are left in the wild. Because there are so many different types of sharks and they are all very different, more research needs to be done. Research about sharks can help people protect them.

I think some people do not want to protect sharks because they are afraid of them. With some sharks being 40 feet long, I'm a little afraid of them, too! When I was at the aquarium, I saw some really big sharks, and I did feel scared. I was glad they were in the water, and I was on the land. Even though sharks live in the ocean and humans live on land, the "Endangered Sharks" article says that scientists think over "100 million sharks are caught and killed each year" by humans. This is a lot of sharks! Although scientists do not know exactly how many sharks are left in the oceans, we do know that 100 million sharks being caught and killed is too many.

There is not a lot people can do to help peregrine falcons anymore. DDT was the main reason they were dying off, and the chemical has been banned. However, there are many things people can do for sharks. By helping people learn about shark fishing and products that might contain sharks, people can help reduce the number being caught and killed each year. According to the "Endangered Sharks" article, "many organizations depend on donations" to help save sharks. The "Saving the Peregrine Falcon" article does not mention organizations needing donations at all.

It seems clear to me that sharks need our help now. The peregrine falcons have already been helped. Our school and community should donate the money to saving the sharks because these animals really need our help.